Catching the Sun

Tales from Asia

Retold by Jan M. Mike

Celebration Press
Pearson Learning Group

Contents

The Fly
A Story of Vietnam

In the poorest of villages near the sea, there lived a peasant with his wife and infant son. The boy had been born in a time of famine. Raging storms had damaged the rice crop and frightened away the fish in the sea. Many people suffered. The peasant was forced to borrow money from his rich neighbor to buy a bit of rice for his wife and baby.

For the next nine years, the peasant worked hard to pay off his debt. Yet each year the neighbor told him he still owed more money. The peasant suspected he'd long ago paid all he owed, but unable to read, he had no way to prove he was being cheated.

One summer day the rich neighbor came again to claim his payment. The young son was alone in the yard.

"Why are you not in school?" the neighbor asked. The boy shrugged. More than anything, he wanted to go to school to learn how to read and write. Then maybe he could prove that his parents had long ago paid their debt. However, as things were, there was no money left to pay for school, or even for paper.

"Well, boy, if you will not tell me why you are not in school, then answer this. Where are your mother and father?" the rich neighbor asked. "I need to find out when they plan to pay me."

The boy wasn't afraid of the powerful neighbor. He knew he had to see if he could outsmart the man.

"My father has gone off to cut down living trees and plant dead ones," the boy said. The rich neighbor looked impatient as the boy continued, "My mother has gone off to sell the wind and buy the moon."

"What is this nonsense?" the neighbor shouted. "Tell me where your parents are, or I will see to it that they punish you."

"Sir, it is not nonsense; it is the truth that I tell you, and my parents would never punish me for telling the truth." The boy stood as he spoke and respectfully bowed to the neighbor.

"Do you know who I am, child?" he asked. "Tell me where your parents are! And this time do not speak in riddles."

Once more the boy said, "My father has gone off to cut down living trees and plant dead ones, and my mother has gone off to sell the wind and buy the moon. There is no riddle, sir."

"I came here today to collect the money your wretched parents owe me. But if you will tell me plainly where they are, I will forgive the debt they owe," the rich neighbor said carefully.

"Sir, why would you make such a joke? Forgive my parents' debt? If only I could believe you." The boy's eyes filled with hope, and he pondered whether he should believe the neighbor. He'd often heard people say the man lied and cheated. Nevertheless, it was hard not to hope that maybe this time he spoke the truth.

If only the man would forget the money his parents owed! Then the family would no longer have to struggle to feed themselves. His father could buy enough land to grow his own rice, and his talented mother could spend her days painting and singing. Most exciting of all, he could go to school!

"Here are heaven and earth to act as witnesses that I tell you the truth," the rich neighbor said slyly.

"Heaven and earth are great indeed," the boy said, "but they cannot testify in court. I would ask for some living thing to be our witness."

"Very well," the neighbor said. He looked around and caught sight of a fly resting on a tall wooden pole. "That fly is a living thing; it will be our witness. Now tell me where your parents are, child, before I get any angrier."

The boy looked at the fly, thought for a moment, and said, "Yes, the fly will be my witness, and I will tell you. My father has taken a job with the farmer. He is cutting down live bamboo and building a fence with it. So, you see, he is cutting down living trees and planting dead ones, as I said."

"Yes, I see; go on." The rich neighbor looked impatient.

"Oh, sir, you will keep your promise, won't you? You will free my parents from the debt that has lasted for so long?"

"Yes, yes, I swear before this fly, child. Now tell me where your mother is. The day grows long and there is much money to be collected and counted."

"Well," said the boy. He took a deep breath. "My mother has gone to the market. There she will sell her beautiful fans to buy oil for our lamp. Is that not selling the wind to buy the moon, sir?"

The rich neighbor laughed aloud. Then he tousled the boy's hair.

"You are a clever young man, but be careful of
being too clever," he said. "You may find that you
have outsmarted yourself one day."

"May I tell my parents that their debt is forgiven?"
the boy asked.

"Tell them. Yes, you should be the one to tell them."
Chuckling, the neighbor turned and strode away.

The boy could hardly wait until his parents came
home so he could give them the good news. How
happy they would be, and how proud!

It was dark by the time his weary mother and father arrived home. The boy had made a simple dinner. After his parents ate, he told them about the rich neighbor's visit.

"Is it true?" his mother asked. "We owe no more money?"

"It's true," the boy declared.

But his father simply said, "We'll see."

Two days later, while the boy was out fishing, the neighbor came to the house once more. When the boy returned home, his father told him about the meeting.

"Our neighbor shouted and told me he had never talked to you and that we still owe him money."

"He is not speaking the truth," the boy said.

"I believe you," his father told him, "but what can we do?"

"We can go to the mandarin," the boy said. The mandarin was a wise man, a judge who was responsible for settling disputes.

"Very well," his father said. "We will take our case to the mandarin."

The boy went inside to cook the fish he'd caught. He felt glad that his father believed and trusted him and knew he would not lie. But could the boy convince the mandarin that he told the truth?

The mandarin's court opened early the next day. The boy stood in the crowd with his parents and listened as the judge patiently decided case after case. The rich neighbor stood nearby, fidgeting impatiently.

"Let us end this foolishness," the boy heard him whisper to a guard. The guard stepped forward and spoke to the mandarin, and their case was called next.

"Tell me exactly what happened," the mandarin said to the boy. The judge's eyes were warm and kind.

The boy took a deep breath and began to speak. Slowly, very slowly, he told the mandarin about the riddle and how the neighbor had agreed his parents owed no more money. Next to him the rich neighbor glared and snorted scornfully. Finally the boy finished his story.

"Lies, all lies!" the neighbor shouted immediately. "That boy should be punished for telling such shocking falsehoods."

The mandarin frowned thoughtfully and turned toward the boy.

"You say this man promised to forgive your parents' debt. Do you have any proof of this claim?" he asked. "Can you even prove that this conversation took place?"

"Oh, yes, Your Honor. There was a witness to his promise."

"And who was this witness?"

"It was a fly, Your Honor."

The mandarin frowned. "A fly! Do you expect me to believe that a fly could be a witness? Do you expect me to call all the flies to court? How ever would we find the right one? How do I even know that a fly was there?"

"What I say is true," the boy declared. "The fly was sitting on our neighbor's nose."

"He lies!" the neighbor shouted. "That fly was sitting on a wooden pole!"

For a moment there was silence. Then all the onlookers burst out laughing. Even the mandarin roared, his thin shoulders shaking under his silk robe. Only the rich neighbor didn't share in the humor. He had been tricked into proving that the boy told the truth.

"You are a clever one," the mandarin told the boy when he'd stopped laughing. "I will keep my eye on you, for one day you may also be a mandarin. A smart boy like you belongs in school."

Then he turned to the rich neighbor, and his smile faded into a somber look. "As for you, your own words convict you. You lied to this boy, to his parents, and to me. You will forgive their debt—and you will bring your scroll to me so that I can see what other lies you have told."

A cheer rang out through the court as the mandarin spoke. The boy's mother reached out and embraced him; his father smiled with pride.

"Now that we are free of debt, we will have enough money to send you to school," he said. He placed a hand on the boy's shoulder. "And that is not all. You may also have relieved others of a great burden of debt today. I think the mandarin is right. You are headed for greatness, my son."

The boy smiled. Maybe he would be a judge someday, but for now he was happy with one thought. He was finally going to school.

Flutter Bird
A Story of India

Deep in the Indian jungle, Flutter Bird skimmed through the air, searching for a particular tree. The tree must be strong and have wide, protective leaves. It was time for Flutter Bird to build a nest and lay her very first eggs. Her small heart was filled with great dreams for her young. How vivid their feathers would be, and how melodious their songs each morning!

Finally the little bird found the perfect tree, one with thick branches and wide green leaves. Towering above the center of the jungle, its boughs were covered with rough, brown bark. In the distance, Flutter Bird heard elephants trumpeting. Such large neighbors would scare away any fierce predators. She'd found the perfect spot for raising her young. Or so she thought.

Flutter Bird built her nest, dreaming of her young. She tucked each twig into place and wrapped her work with sturdy vines. She lined the bottom of the nest with her own soft, downy feathers. She laid her eggs, one each day for four days. Then she spread her wings protectively and waited for them to hatch.

A week or so later, Grandfather Elephant pounded into the jungle on his daily walk. Raising his trunk, he trumpeted loudly. Small animals, birds, and insects huddled in fear as he stomped past.

Flutter Bird watched in horror as he advanced toward her nesting tree. She cried, "Grandfather Elephant, please do not shake this tree."

Grandfather Elephant did not even hear her. The afternoon was hot, and his thick, gray skin itched fiercely so that all he wanted was to scratch. He slammed into Flutter Bird's tree with such force that the jungle shook. Her nest tilted wildly, and she flapped her wings in panic.

"Have mercy, Grandfather Elephant!" she sang out. "My nest will fall. My beautiful eggs will break."

Grandfather Elephant was not listening. Again he rammed his boulder-sized head into the tree, scratching the delicate space between his ears. Then he rubbed his side against the rough bark.

The huge tree shook and swayed, and Flutter Bird's nest fell to the ground. She screeched and swooped down, flapping her wings in pain and anger.

"My children! You thoughtless beast, what have you done to my children?" She pecked at the delicate bits of eggshell and cried for her broken dreams.

Grandfather Elephant paid no attention. The jungle teemed with small creatures. None of them was worth bothering about. He shook his head, snorted, and lumbered off through the jungle.

Flutter Bird cried out as the great elephant walked away, "You have made an enemy, Elephant. Small as I am, I will make you hear me."

Then she sped off to find her friend Yellow Parrot, who lived in a nearby tree. "Grandfather Elephant has destroyed my eggs," she said. "Help me teach him not to ignore us as he stomps through the jungle."

"That old elephant is a menace. He knocked down my favorite tree last month," Yellow Parrot replied. She shook her head and then preened her bright chest feathers, looking thoughtful.

Flutter Bird watched her hopefully. The parrot was the oldest, wisest bird in the jungle. Surely she would know what to do.

"Grandfather Elephant is large and strong. We will need a clever plan to stop him," Yellow Parrot finally said. "Striped Bee is wise in the ways of the jungle. Let's find her and ask for her help."

The two birds flew to the east, where the morning sun first lights the sky. There Striped Bee had built her nest in the honey tree.

As Flutter Bird told her woeful tale, Striped Bee hovered near, shaking her head with sorrow.

"Can you help us, Striped Bee?" Parrot asked.

"I will help you all I can," buzzed the bee. "Grandfather Elephant has destroyed many of our precious hives. None of us is safe until he learns to respect all the animals."

The two birds nodded in agreement. Striped Bee buzzed thoughtfully for a moment and then continued. "My friend Green Frog lives in the pond beyond the rice fields," she said. "She hears all that goes on in the jungle. Perhaps she can help us."

The three companions flew off to Green Frog's pond, where the air was filled with the rich scent of lotus blossoms.

"Green Frog," Striped Bee called out. Grandfather Elephant has destroyed Flutter Bird's home and broken her eggs. She begged him to take care, but he paid no attention. Can you help us teach him not to harm the smaller animals who live here?"

Green Frog answered, "I have heard many tales of Grandfather Elephant's carelessness. You know how all frogs love to gossip, calling to one another all evening long. I agree; it is time we taught him to be more respectful. I believe I have a plan that may solve our problem—if we all work together." The others listened carefully while Green Frog explained her plan.

The next day Flutter Bird watched as Grandfather Elephant began his daily walk. Her heart pounded with fearful determination as she waited, peering out from behind a flowering bush.

"Be patient," a chorus of nearby frogs croaked softly. "We are waiting to help you."

Finally Grandfather Elephant lumbered into the jungle, trailed by Flutter Bird and Yellow Parrot. As usual he paid no attention to them.

Because of the great heat, he never noticed how quiet the jungle was, or how still the air. Most of the small animals knew of the plan and were hiding. When he was far enough into the jungle, Striped Bee and her hive mates buzzed around his face.

He shook his head, trying to frighten them away, but it did no good. In a dazzling dance of flight, the bees stayed close to the beast's big, floppy, sensitive ears.

Grandfather Elephant beat the ground with his huge feet, raising a cloud of blinding dust just as Flutter Bird and Yellow Parrot landed on his tossing head. Holding tight, they fanned the rising dust into his eyes. He swung his trunk and bellowed in fury.

Blinded by the dust, he bounded through the jungle, trying to escape his tiny tormentors. Through the buzzing by his ears, Grandfather Elephant finally heard a chorus of frogs croaking nearby, and he knew that frogs meant water. Water would cool his itchy skin and chase away the bees. He could fill his trunk with water and spray the annoying birds that fanned dust into his eyes. With a loud bellow he galloped toward the croaking sounds.

However, there was no cool water, only a long, deep hole that a hunter had dug the day before. The enormous elephant slipped and slid to the bottom. He was trapped.

Grandfather Elephant could not open his stinging eyes. He shook his head and stomped his feet.

"Someone! Help!" he trumpeted. "Come and get me out of this trap."

"You crushed my nest and destroyed my eggs," Flutter Bird whistled into his ear. "I begged you to be careful. Why should I help you?"

"You tore down my favorite tree," Yellow Parrot chattered. "Why should I help you?"

"You destroyed my precious hives," Striped Bee buzzed angrily. "Why should I help you?"

"You are a menace to all the small animals of the jungle," Green Frog croaked from the edge of the pit. "Why should we help a dangerous bully like you?"

The giant elephant tried to open his smarting eyes. He attempted to climb the sides of the pit, but again and again he slipped back into the muddy hole.

Finally Grandfather Elephant gave up. He hung his head. A single tear dripped from one small eye.

"Well?" said Yellow Parrot. The silence grew as the friends waited for an answer.

"Please forgive me," the elephant finally said, hanging his trunk in sorrow. "I never realized the harm I was doing."

"I am pleased that you finally hear us," Green Frog croaked, "but you must do more. You must tell the other elephants. Train them all to listen to the small voices of the jungle. If you promise to do that, we will lead you out of this hole."

Grandfather Elephant promised. Yellow Parrot and Flutter Bird filled their beaks with clear water at a nearby spring. Carefully they rinsed the blinding dust from his sore eyes. The birds and frogs and bees guided Grandfather Elephant along the side of the pit to a spot where he could climb out. He walked, more carefully now, back to his herd.

So it was that Grandfather Elephant learned his lesson. *Listen to those who are smaller than you. Together they are much stronger than you might think.*

The Moon Weaver
A Story of China

Many years ago, when the moon was young, there lived a poor peasant named Yuang Shuai. He owned a small plot of rocky land outside the city. With his ox he worked the rugged land, growing what little he could.

Yuang Shuai worked hard and was often weary. Nevertheless, once every week he walked to the city. There he would stroll through the markets, hoping to find a woman to love and marry.

One evening like any other, Yuang Shuai walked home from the city beneath the light of the full moon. Out in the forest he heard a loud splash and a cry for help. Quickly he raced toward the sound. A small, flat pond of water shimmered in the moonlight near the edge of a meadow. There, near a rock, Yuang Shuai saw what looked like a small heap of shivering silk. As he crept toward the silk, he realized that it was a woman and that she was weeping.

"Forgive me," he said, touching her shoulder. "Are you hurt?"

The woman's face was round and sweet like the moon. Tear tracks glistened beneath her eyes.

"Oh, it is you," she said. "I hoped you would find me."

Yuang Shuai was puzzled. He had never seen this woman before. Surely he would remember such grace and beauty. Nonetheless, she needed help, so he carried her, cold and shivering, to his house.

Wrapped in a warm blanket, the young woman drank hot tea. Then she spoke, her voice soft and low. "I am Yi Llian, a Moon Weaver. For many years I have watched you go each week to and from the city. Gradually I grew to understand that you are a good man and that I care deeply for you."

She asked for more tea and then continued, "So I leapt upon a spark of starlight and traveled down to meet you. But I fell into something wet."

"The pond," Yuang Shuai said.

Yi Llian nodded thoughtfully. "The pond—yes, I fell into the pond. Then I was wet and cold. I have never felt such things before."

Yuang Shuai smiled uncertainly. "I see. Tell me, what is a Moon Weaver?"

"My sisters and I weave the silver rays of moonlight. The moon is a very proud and demanding mistress. She must have only the best, and I am the most skilled of all her weavers. My sisters are quite happy living in her beautiful palace, but I have wanted to leave for many years, even before I noticed you."

"Ah, I see," said Yuang Shuai. In truth, he did not understand at all. Was this woman mad, with her talk of palaces in the sky and weaving moonlight?

It did not matter if she was, he realized, for he had found the lovely woman he wanted to marry. Or more precisely, she had found him.

They were married the next day at a small temple in the city. In the next weeks Yi Llian set up a stall to sell her weaving. With the money she earned, they built a small house. Word of her glorious weaving spread near and far, and soon she had many customers.

As Yi Llian's business grew, so did the couple's happiness. With happiness came two children. The first was a boy named Yuang Jing, and the second was a girl called Li Pei. Life was filled with contentment and harmony. However, in all their time together, never once did Yi Llian go out after dark.

"The moon is a jealous mistress. If she sees me, she will want me back," she told her husband.

He simply nodded and said nothing.

One night the bright autumn moon glowed in the sky, and the evening breeze blew soft and cool.

"Come walk with us to the river," Yuang Shuai said to his wife.

"I should not," Yi Llian said, but Yuang Shuai could tell that she wanted to. He took her by the hand.

"Li Pei and Yuang Jing are waiting for us. I promised them we would go for a walk together, and I always keep my promises." He smiled at her and kissed her forehead.

"By now the moon must have forgotten me," Yi Llian said with a smile. "I will walk with you and the children, just to the river and back."

They walked, laughing and talking, under the pale, silver light of the moon and stars. Li Pei rode on her father's shoulders, and Yuang Jing held his mother's hand.

As they reached the riverbank, Yi Llian looked up at Li Pei, smiled, and wiped a smudge of dirt off the little girl's chin. Then she stopped suddenly.

All around Yi Llian the air began to glow. As her family watched in horror, sparkling rays of silver light shot down from the moon, covering her from head to toes.

"No!" she cried out. "It is the moon; she is taking me back!"

"Yi Llian!" Yuang Shuai tried to grab her, but his hands slid right off her. "Stay with us. Don't go!"

"I want to stay," she called, as the glowing light transported her into the air.

"I will come for you; I promise!" Yuang Shuai shouted as his wife rose up, up into the night sky.

Then she was gone. Li Pei and Yuang Jing began to cry bitterly as they walked home. The house was dark and silent without Yi Llian.

The next morning Yuang Shuai packed food and warm clothing into two baskets, which he put on a carrying pole. On each basket he set one of the children. Then he lifted the pole to his shoulders and left the house.

"We are going to get your mother," Yuang Shuai told the children.

"How will we find her?" Li Pei asked.

Yuang Shuai did not answer. But he knew he had to try to get his wife back from the moon.

There was a steep mountain beyond the city. Perhaps there would be something on top of the mountain, some way to reach up to the moon and pull Yi Llian home. Yuang Shuai decided he would start there.

The sun was setting when they reached the base of the mountain. Yuang Shuai began to climb just as the cold, hard disk of the moon appeared over the cliffs. An icy wind began to blow and seemed to come directly from the angry moon. It was clear to Yuang Shuai that the moon would not give up her favorite moon weaver easily.

The children huddled down in the baskets, shivering. Yuang Shuai was weary, but he climbed on. Soon the wind turned to rain—first light drizzle and then an icy downpour. The silver moon peered down through the storm, a watchful eye in the night sky.

Yuang Shuai hesitated. Now the rain had made the rocks slippery. Perhaps he should take the children home and try again in daylight when the moon was less strong.

As if they knew what he was thinking, the children cried out, urging him to go on.

"The way is difficult," he said. "The rocks are slippery and the path is steep."

"Please go on!" they shouted back.

Near the top of the mountain, the rain became a
torrent. Water fell in waves, cascading down the
jagged rocks. Again Yuang Shuai hesitated, and again
the children pleaded with him to keep climbing.

Finally he climbed over the last large boulders
near the top of the mountain. Off in the distance he
saw ribbons of moonlight, shimmering behind the
storm. A river of water, fed by the pouring rain,
churned across the mountaintop, between the
frightened family and the moonlight.

Yuang Shuai put down the carrying pole and stared at the water. It was too deep to walk across and far too wild to swim through. What could he do?

The children thought they knew. They ran toward the water carrying empty clay pots. Li Pei and Yuang Jing filled the pots with water, and then they dumped the water over the edge of the mountain.

Yuang Shuai shook his head in sorrow for his poor, motherless children. It would be impossible to carry all that water and pour it off the mountain. Yet there was nothing else to try, no other way to make it across, and standing still would do no good.

So as rain lashed his shivering body, Yuang Shuai grabbed the largest of the pots. He filled it and then poured the water off the side of the mountain. Over and over, pot by pot, hopeless as it seemed, he and the children tried to empty the raging river.

Suddenly Li Pei shouted and pointed. As Yuang Shuai looked up, the rain stopped, and soft moonbeams formed a stairway of shimmering light. There, walking slowly down the silver stairway, was Yi Llian.

Without rain to feed it, the river trickled away down the mountain. Yuang Jing and Li Pei ran to their mother, and she took them in her arms. Yuang Shuai quickly approached.

"What happened?" he asked his wife.

"At first the moon was furious," she answered. "That is why she sent the storms against you. But as she watched my family try so hard to reach me, her hard heart softened. Finally she had her weavers make this stairway, and she sent me back to you."

Yi Llian and her family went safely home that very night. Of course, this all happened very long ago, and some say it is just a story. Only the moon knows for certain, and she will never tell.

Maui and the Sun
A Story of Polynesia

Did you see the sun today as she slid over the horizon? Did you observe her as she moved slowly, oh so slowly and queenlike across the sky? "No need to watch," you say? "The sun moves slowly across the sky every day, and there is sunlight enough for work and for play." That is true, my friend, but it was not always so.

37

When the sun was young, she was like a small child racing across the sky, not thinking about the people below. Some days were short, others were shorter, and a few were so short that they were over almost as soon as they began.

A young person might get out of bed when the sun rose and quickly sit down to a breakfast of coconut meat and sago biscuits. Then there would barely be time to run outside and gather friends, choose a game, and agree on the rules, when *whoosh!* The sun was already setting, and the day was over before the children got a chance to play the game.

There was not enough sunlight for people to do their work. There was not enough sunlight for fishing or for beating bark from the paper mulberry tree into tapa cloth for beautiful skirts or for grinding taro root into flour. The situation made everyone feel upset. Everyone grumbled, but what could anyone do?

In this long ago time, in a little village in Manihiki, there was a family that was blessed with many children. First a boy was born. He grew tall and strong, and his parents were very proud of him. He was the eldest child in his family, though no one remembers his name, I am sad to say.

Four more brothers followed, each one tall and each one smart. Then a sister was born. Her name was Hina, and she was also tall, straight, and strong—stronger even than any of her brothers. Her long, shining black hair swept the ground when she walked.

Finally came one last boy, who was named Maui. He was not the strongest, but he was very clever. Maui the trickster he was called. It was he who tamed the sun and made her move more slowly and set the length of our days. This is how it happened.

One day Maui and his brothers decided to go fishing, far out in the deep waters of the ocean. Hina came with them to steer the boat and cheer them with her songs. Out toward the deepest parts of the sea, the brothers paddled, and then they dropped their hooks into the water.

Without warning, the sun plunged over the edge of the ocean, leaving them in the cold and dark.

"This foolishness has gone on long enough," Maui said, as they paddled rapidly for home. "We must teach the sun to move slowly across the sky."

"No one can teach the sun anything," his eldest brother said. "If it could be done, someone would have done it already. Therefore it cannot be done."

"It can be done," said Maui, "and we will do it. I have a plan."

Maui showed his brothers how to twist coconut fibers into sturdy ropes. Hina sat beside them, singing and braiding her long, long hair. Maui and his brothers made a loop with a long rope. Then they fastened six long ropes to the loop—one for each of the brothers.

Back they paddled, out to the deep pit at the far edge of the ocean, where the sun goes each night to sleep. In the dark they paddled, with only the sound of the splashing waves, Hina's singing, and the grumbling of all the brothers.

"This is foolish, Maui."

"This is dangerous, Maui."

"We will be eaten by sharks, Maui."

"We will fall over the edge, Maui."

"It cannot be done, for if it could be done, someone would have done it. No one can catch the sun, Maui."

But Maui just said, "Hold on tight to your ropes!" As the sun rose from her bed, Maui threw the large loop of rope.

The sun was trapped, but not for long. How she struggled! She fought harder than the biggest fish. Then *whoomp,* the rope broke, and the sun was free again.

"We told you it could not be done, Maui," all five brothers said at once.

"We will try again," was Maui's answer.

Home they paddled through the black night. The next morning Maui told the brothers to gather more coconut fibers. They collected every bit of fiber they could find on the island. They twisted these new fibers into stronger, thicker ropes.

Then Hina taught her brothers how to braid. Each brother braided three strong ropes into one that was even stronger. Once again Maui and his brothers made a large loop and fastened six ropes to it.

The brothers did not want to try again, but Maui insisted and Maui prodded. Out they paddled again in the cold gloom while Hina sang and the five brothers continued to grumble.

"We are sure it cannot be done," the five brothers said all together to Maui.

"Hold your ropes tight," was all Maui said, and he paddled even harder. To the very edge of the ocean he paddled, and there he tossed the loop across the pit where the sun liked to sleep.

They waited silently in the cold night, using their paddles to keep back from the watery pit and steadying the rope. Then a blinding light hit their eyes. The sun rose with a loud *whoosh!* and headed into the rope trap. Caught, she struggled and burned so bright that the ropes caught fire and fell away. Then the sun streaked away across the sky.

"We told you it could not be done, Maui," all five brothers said together.

"We will try again," was Maui's answer.

Back to the island they paddled, but there was no more coconut fiber to twist into ropes. Maui knew what he had to do, though it made him sad.

"We need your hair," he said to Hina, looking into her eyes, "your beautiful, long hair."

"I was waiting for you to ask," was all Hina said.

"Teach us how to weave a net," Maui added, "and this time you will hold it with us."

Hina quickly cut off all of her long, black, glorious hair. Then she taught her brothers how to weave a net.

Oh, what a net they wove from her hair! More delicate than a spider web, it stretched across the island like a lacy flower vine.

The net looked easily broken, but it was very strong, like Hina. Carefully she carried it onto the boat.

The canoe went back into the water, as once more the brothers and sister paddled to the edge of the ocean. Once again the five brothers grumbled.

"The net is too fragile, Maui."

"The net is too small, Maui."

"The net will burn like the ropes, Maui."

"The sun will squeeze through the holes, Maui."

"It cannot be done, for if it could be done, someone would have done it. No one can catch the sun, Maui."

"Hold the net," Maui said. "It is strong, just as Hina is strong. It will capture the sun."

Maui tossed the net across the pit, just as the sun streaked into the sky. Maui, Hina, and their brothers gripped that delicate net as tightly as bark grips a tree. How the sun fought to be free! She tugged against the net and thrashed about. The waves rose high. The little boat bounced, slapped down, rocked, and bucked—but the net did not break. Maui, Hina, and the brothers all held onto it with all their might.

The sun burned bright and hot, and every hair in
the net turned a brilliant color—peach and gold, red
and coral, orange and violet. The net blazed with
light, but it did not burn. At long last they had
caught the sun.

"Let me go," cried the sun, when she realized she
could not escape.

"We'll let you go, but first you must make a
promise," Maui shouted.

Sizzling and popping and shouting like an angry
child, the sun asked, "What promise must I make?"

"Each day you must peek over the edge of the ocean very slowly. Each day you must creep across the sky very, very slowly like a turtle carrying a heavy shell. When it is time to set, you must move more slowly still, so every person and every animal will know that night is about to descend."

The sun sulked and brooded and whined and blustered, but nothing persuaded Maui to release her. Finally, convinced she could not win, she gave in.

"I will make you that promise," the sun said.

Maui, Hina, and the five brothers let go of the net. Slowly, very slowly, the sun began to move, the net trailing beside her and lighting the sky.

"Ha! We told you all along that it could be done, Maui," all five brothers said, as they clapped one another on the back in triumph. For that was how they remembered it, of course.

"What will we do tomorrow, Maui?" the eldest brother asked.

"Climb the mountains?"

"Swim down below the coral reefs?"

"Tame the winds of the typhoon?"

The brothers pelted him with questions, but Maui just smiled and gazed upward as the sun rose ever so slowly in the sky.

Ah, you smile and shake your head, but this tale is true. The net that was Hina's hair still encircles and trails the sun to this very day.

Look for yourself. You can see the net best when the sun first rises at dawn or when she sinks beyond the edge of the earth at sunset. Peach and gold, red and coral, orange and violet—Hina's hair shimmers in the sky.